D0992488

HIP-HOP DANCING

POPPING, LOCKING,

AND EVERYTHING IN BETWEEN

VOLUME 3

by Wendy Garofoli

Consultant:
AleKsa "LeX" Chmiel, Co-Director/Owner
Flomotion Dance Company
Philadelphia, Pennsylvania

CAPSTONE PRESS
a capstone imprint

Velocity is published by Capstone Press,
151 Good Counsel Drive, P.O. Box 669, Mankato, Minnesota 56002.
www.capstonepub.com

Books published by Capstone Press are manufactured with paper
containing at least 10 percent post-consumer waste.

Library of Congress Cataloging-in-Publication Data
Garofoli, Wendy.
 Hip-hop dancing / by Wendy Garofoli.
 p. cm.
 Includes bibliographical references and index.
 Summary: "Provides step-by-step instructions for learning breaking, popping, locking,
and krumping hip-hop dance moves"—Provided by publisher.
 ISBN 978-1-4296-5484-5 (library binding)—ISBN 978-1-4296-5485-2 (library
binding)—ISBN 978-1-4296-5486-9 (library binding)—ISBN 978-1-4296-5487-6
(library binding)
 1. Hip-hop dance. I. Title.
 GV1796.H57G37 2011
 793.3—dc22   2010030394

Editorial Credits
Megan Peterson and Jennifer Besel, editors; Veronica Correia, designer; Marcie Spence,
    media researcher; Sarah Schuette, photo stylist; Laura Manthe, production specialist

Photo Credits
Capstone Studio: 6 (top), Karon Dubke, cover, 5, 12, 13, 18 (bottom), 19, 24, 25, 26
(bottom), 28, 29, 34, 35, 42, 43, 44, 45 (top), TJ Thoraldson Digital Photography, 8-9,
10, 11, 14, 15, 16, 17, 18 (top), 20, 21, 22, 23, 26 (top), 27, 30, 31, 32, 33, 36, 37, 38,
39, 40, 41; Getty Images, Inc.: John Rogers, 7; iStockphoto Inc.: AleksandarGeorgiev, 6
(background), caracterdesign, 6 (bottom); Shutterstock: Andrei Nekrassov, 45 (bottom),
skvoor, 4

Printed in the United States of America in Stevens Point, Wisconsin.
092010
005934WZS11

TABLE OF CONTENTS

INTRO   FROM THE WEST 4

CHAPTER 1   POPPING MOVES 10

CHAPTER 2   LOCKING MOVES 20

CHAPTER 3   THE ROBOT 32

CHAPTER 4   WAVING AND TUTTING 34

CHAPTER 5   GLIDING, FLOATING, AND SLIDING . . 38

GLOSSARY 46
READ MORE 47
INTERNET SITES 47
INDEX 48

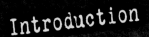

FROM THE WEST

Sharp muscle ticks. Over-the-top arm movements. Smooth footwork. Many people have heard of the hip-hop dance styles called popping and locking. These styles are performed on TV, in movies, and in dance studios around the world. But many people don't know that popping and locking got their start on the West Coast in the 1960s and 1970s.

popping—sharp ticks of the muscles; invented in the mid-1970s by Sam "Boogaloo Sam" Solomon in Fresno, California

Fresno, CA

locking—bold, playful movements; invented in the late 1960s by Don Campbell in Los Angeles

Los Angeles, CA

Popping and locking are just two of the many types of hip-hop dances that were developed on the West Coast. These dances are called the funk styles. The funk styles also include gliding, waving, tutting, the robot, and many more. Each of these styles has its own technique. But there is one rule when performing funk—dance with style!

GET FUNKY

The funk styles were first performed to funk music. Funk music is a blend of soul music, jazz, and R&B. Artists such as James Brown, Parliament, Funkadelic, Rick James, and World Class Wreckin' Cru were popular with old-school poppers and lockers. Dancers continue to get down to these funk artists today. But there's no rule that says you must dance the funk styles to funk music. You can pop or lock to any song as long as it has a solid beat and heavy bass.

GEAR

In order to practice the funk styles, you'll need to wear the right gear:

- loose-fitting T-shirt and sweatpants for ease of movement
- sneakers with smooth soles that let you easily slide across the floor during glide moves
- knee pads to protect your knees during floor work

COSTUMING

When performing the funk styles, you may choose to wear a specific costume:

○ Popping Costumes: Old-school poppers wore dress shoes and pin-striped suits to accent the sharpness of their moves.

○ Locking Costumes: Old-school lockers wore over-the-top, colorful costumes that included striped knee socks, knickers, suspenders, and gloves.

The clothing styles of the old-school lockers influence hip-hop artists today.

WORK IT OUT

Popping requires that you **isolate** certain muscles. Strengthening those muscles will make you a better popper. And all funk styles require **agility**. It's important to stretch before you try any of them. Here are a few exercises to get you started:

SHOULDERS: Stretch your right arm across your chest. Hold it against your chest with your left hand for about 30 seconds. Repeat with the left arm.

NECK: Tilt your head slowly to the right and left. Tilt your chin upward, and then slowly lower your chin into your chest. Then turn your head to the right and left.

QUADRICEPS: Start in a standing position. Hold onto a wall or piece of furniture for support. Bend your right knee, and grab your right foot behind you. Try to touch your right foot to your backside without arching your back. Repeat with your left foot.

HAMSTRINGS: Sit on the floor with your legs extended straight in front of you. Reach forward to your toes. Point your toes and try to touch your stomach to your legs. Then flex your feet.

ARMS AND BACK: Do a set of push-ups, keeping your stomach flat and your legs straight behind you. Start with 10 push-ups, and then work your way up.

STOMACH: Do a set of sit-ups or crunches. Start with 25 sit-ups. Then work your way up.

isolate–*to highlight a particular muscle or area of the body separate from the others*
agility–*the ability to move fast and easily*

Chapter 1

POPPING MOVES

Neck-o-Flex

DIFFICULTY: ⭐☆

The Neck-o-Flex is a basic popping move. With a twist of the neck and turn of the body, you can wow audiences. They'll think your head and body are moving separately from each other!

Step 1

Stand in a relaxed position with your feet side by side. Turn your head to the left. Don't tilt your chin up or down.

Step 2

Keep your head in place, and turn your body so it's facing the opposite direction. Step with your left foot, and **pivot** on your right heel. Your chin is now positioned above your right shoulder. Your body faces the opposite direction as in Step 1.

pivot—to turn suddenly as if on a central point

Step 3

Turn your head to the left.

Step 4

Keep your head in place and turn your body to the left. Your chin is now positioned above your right shoulder. Your body faces the same direction as in Step 1.

Boogaloo Sam

As locking gained popularity in the mid-1970s, a dancer named Sam "Boogaloo Sam" Solomon developed his own dance style. Sam isolated his muscles in small, short bursts. Each time he hit a new position, he said "pop." That's how the style of popping got its name. Boogaloo Sam went on to form a dance group called the Electronic Boogaloo Lockers, later known as the Electric Boogaloos. He is credited with creating popping, as well as a related dance style called boogaloo. Boogaloo is a loose type of dance that makes it appear as though the body has no skeleton. Some popping moves, such as the Old Man, are also considered boogaloo moves.

WALKOUT

DIFFICULTY: ★☆

The Walkout is an important **transition** move that poppers use between bigger, showier steps. Poppers perform the Walkout as they come on stage. They also use the move as they get ready for a **battle**.

Step 1

Stand with your feet together and arms at your sides. Lift both arms straight out in front of you. At the same time, step in front of your left foot with your right foot. As you step across, turn your head, torso, and arms to the right.

Twist your head, torso, and arms to the left.

Step 2

Step back to the right with your right foot, keeping the toes turned out. Land with your feet wider apart than your shoulders. At the same time, turn your head, torso, and arms to the left.

transition—*a step performed in order to move from one dance step to another*
battle—*a competition between individual dancers or groups*

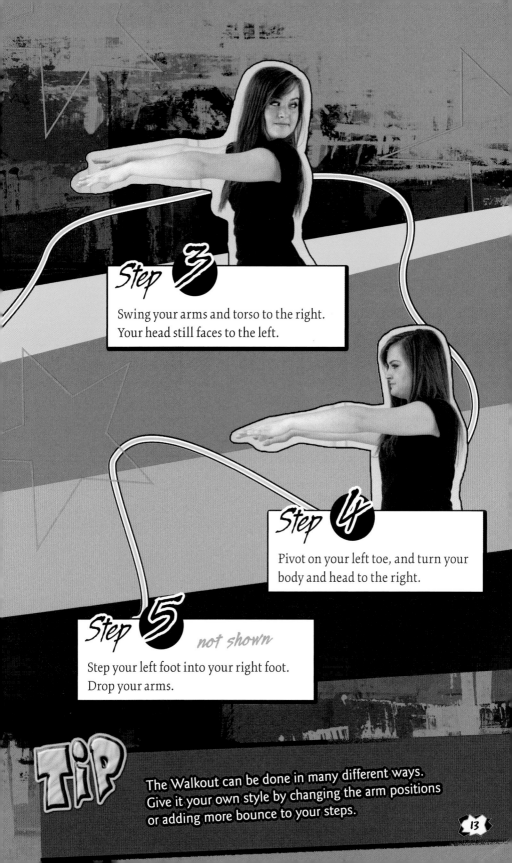

Step 3

Swing your arms and torso to the right. Your head still faces to the left.

Step 4

Pivot on your left toe, and turn your body and head to the right.

Step 5 *not shown*

Step your left foot into your right foot. Drop your arms.

TIP

The Walkout can be done in many different ways. Give it your own style by changing the arm positions or adding more bounce to your steps.

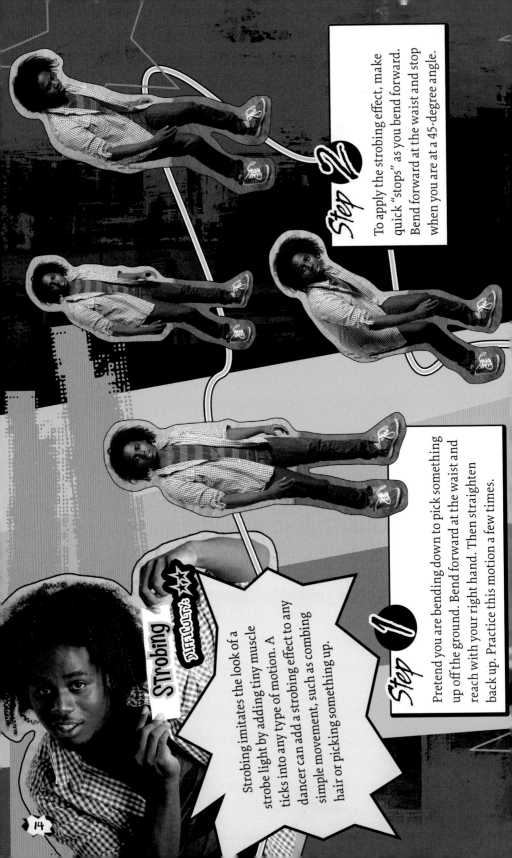

Strobing

DIFFICULT: ★★★☆☆

Strobing imitates the look of a strobe light by adding tiny muscle ticks into any type of motion. A dancer can add a strobing effect to any simple movement, such as combing hair or picking something up.

Step 1

Pretend you are bending down to pick something up off the ground. Bend forward at the waist and reach with your right hand. Then straighten back up. Practice this motion a few times.

Step 2

To apply the strobing effect, make quick "stops" as you bend forward. Bend forward at the waist and stop when you are at a 45-degree angle.

Step 3

Bend forward a bit more and start to reach with your hand. Stop when your back is parallel to the ground.

Tip

As you become more comfortable with strobing, you can add more stops between your movements. Each stop should feel more like a pause than an actual popping of the body.

Step 4

Bend forward even more. Stop when your hand just about reaches the object you are picking up.

Step 5

Repeat these stops on the way back up.

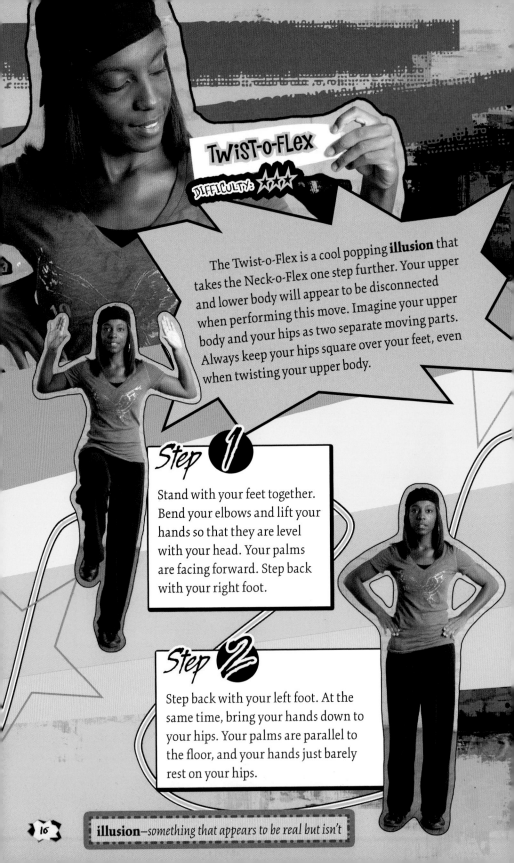

TWiST-O-FLEX

DIFFICULTY: ★★★

The Twist-o-Flex is a cool popping **illusion** that takes the Neck-o-Flex one step further. Your upper and lower body will appear to be disconnected when performing this move. Imagine your upper body and your hips as two separate moving parts. Always keep your hips square over your feet, even when twisting your upper body.

Step 1

Stand with your feet together. Bend your elbows and lift your hands so that they are level with your head. Your palms are facing forward. Step back with your right foot.

Step 2

Step back with your left foot. At the same time, bring your hands down to your hips. Your palms are parallel to the floor, and your hands just barely rest on your hips.

illusion—*something that appears to be real but isn't*

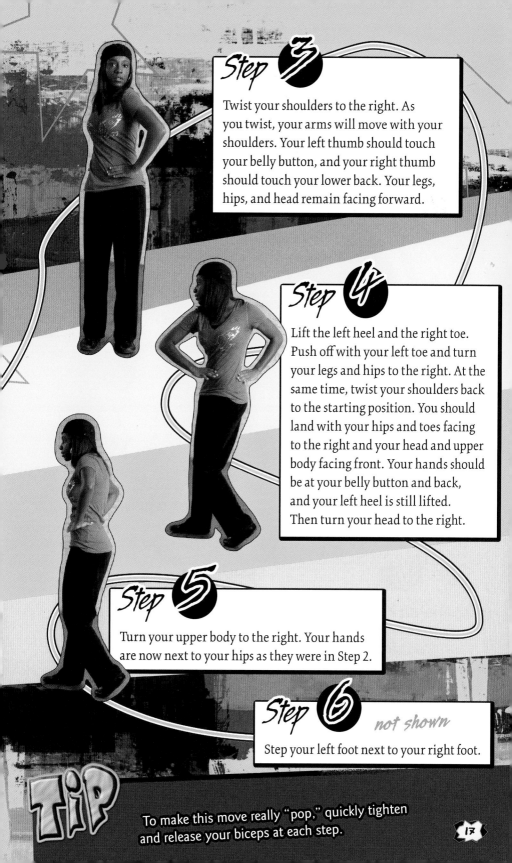

Step 3

Twist your shoulders to the right. As you twist, your arms will move with your shoulders. Your left thumb should touch your belly button, and your right thumb should touch your lower back. Your legs, hips, and head remain facing forward.

Step 4

Lift the left heel and the right toe. Push off with your left toe and turn your legs and hips to the right. At the same time, twist your shoulders back to the starting position. You should land with your hips and toes facing to the right and your head and upper body facing front. Your hands should be at your belly button and back, and your left heel is still lifted. Then turn your head to the right.

Step 5

Turn your upper body to the right. Your hands are now next to your hips as they were in Step 2.

Step 6
not shown

Step your left foot next to your right foot.

Tip

To make this move really "pop," quickly tighten and release your biceps at each step.

Old Man

DIFFICULTY: ★★☆

The Old Man is designed to look as though you are an old person wobbling along. But to pull it off, you actually have to be really **limber**! You'll be rolling your torso around in a circle as you move your feet and hips. First learn the feet and hip movements. Add the torso rolls once you've mastered the basics.

Step 1

Stand with feet slightly apart. Kick your right foot forward and then swing it around to the right side. Land with your feet apart, a bit wider than your shoulders. As your right foot lands, bend your left knee and lean to the left, raising your left arm up. Your arm should look relaxed, as though you are leaning on a counter.

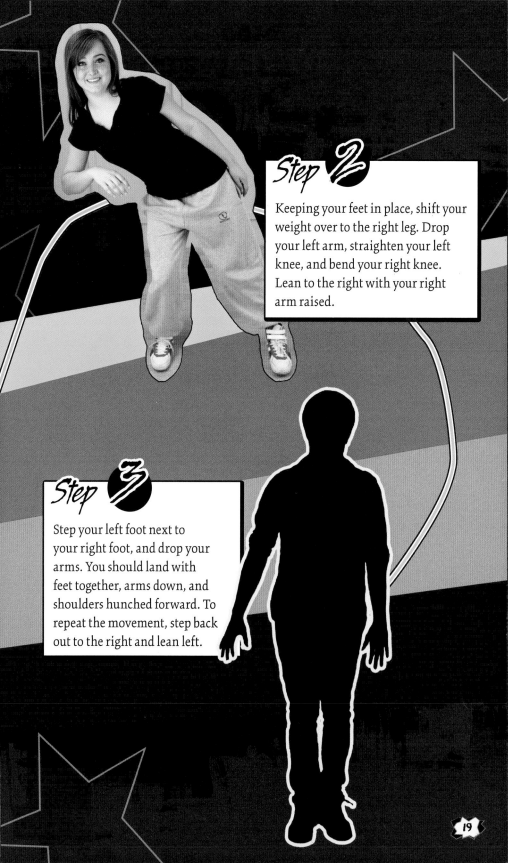

Step 2

Keeping your feet in place, shift your weight over to the right leg. Drop your left arm, straighten your left knee, and bend your right knee. Lean to the right with your right arm raised.

Step 3

Step your left foot next to your right foot, and drop your arms. You should land with feet together, arms down, and shoulders hunched forward. To repeat the movement, step back out to the right and lean left.

Chapter 2

LOCKING MOVES

Wrist Twirls

DIFFICULTY: ☆

Lockers add simple arm movements called Wrist Twirls to many of their moves. Wrist Twirls involve rolling the wrists away from and into the body.

Step 1

Stand with your hands in fists and arms by your sides.

TIP

To bring your arms back down, reverse the Wrist Twirl. Roll your wrists in toward your body. Finish the move with your arms by your sides.

Raise your arms in front of your body. As you raise your arms, roll your wrists by turning out your palms. Your palms should now face away from your body.

Step 3

When you end the move, your fists should be close together above your head, and your elbows should be bent. Your arms should make a diamond shape.

Origins of Locking

In the late 1960s, Don Campbell had trouble remembering the moves to a popular dance called the funky chicken. He kept freezing, or "locking," in place in the middle of his moves. When he made a mistake, he played it off by pointing to the audience and laughing along with them. Later those locks and points became the foundation for the locking dance style.

Scooby Doo

DIFFICULTY: ★★☆

The Scooby Doo allows you to put together a few basic locking movements. You'll be kicking, jumping, and, of course, locking, all in a few simple steps.

Step 1

Stand in a relaxed position with feet together and arms at your sides. Hold your hands in fists. Complete a Wrist Twirl.

Step 2

Roll your wrists back down so your arms are at your sides. Then hit a lock position by bending your elbows and knees, hunching your shoulders, and turning out your toes.

Step 3

Return to a standing position. At the same time, kick your right foot forward, scuffing your heel along the ground.

Step 4

Lift the right knee and jump up off your left foot. As you jump, you will bend the left knee as well. Land first with your right foot and then with your left. Do not land with both feet at the same time.

TiP

Be sure to start and land any jump with bent knees. Landing on straight knees puts too much pressure on your knees and could result in injury.

Whichaway

DIFFICULTY: ⭐⭐☆

In the Whichaway, the dancer kicks one leg at a time. The result is a funky kick that looks like a clock pendulum swinging from side to side.

Step 1

Stand in a relaxed position with your hands clasped together in front of you.

Step 2

Hop onto your left foot, and lift your right knee.

Step 3

Kick out your right foot behind you. Pivot slightly on your left toes so your body faces to the left.

Step 4

Lift your right knee to the right side. As you lift your knee, pivot your body until it faces straight forward.

Step 5

Kick your right leg straight out to the right. Then swing it down to the ground.

Step 6

As your right foot lands, kick your left foot behind you. Your body now faces slightly to the right.

Step 7

Lift your left knee to the left side. As you lift your knee, pivot so your body faces straight forward.

Step 8

Kick your left leg straight out to the left. Then swing it down to the ground.

Tip

Each time you bend your knee at the top of the leg swing, lift it as close to your shoulder as you can.

Scoobot

DIFFICULTY: ★★

The Scoobot involves fairly simple footwork that's performed at a fast pace. What makes it a tricky move are the Wrist Twirls that accompany each kick and step.

Step 1

Stand with your feet together. Your arms are by your sides with hands in fists. Kick your right leg to the side. Keep your leg angled toward the ground. At the same time, roll your left wrist up above your head, and extend your right arm out to the right.

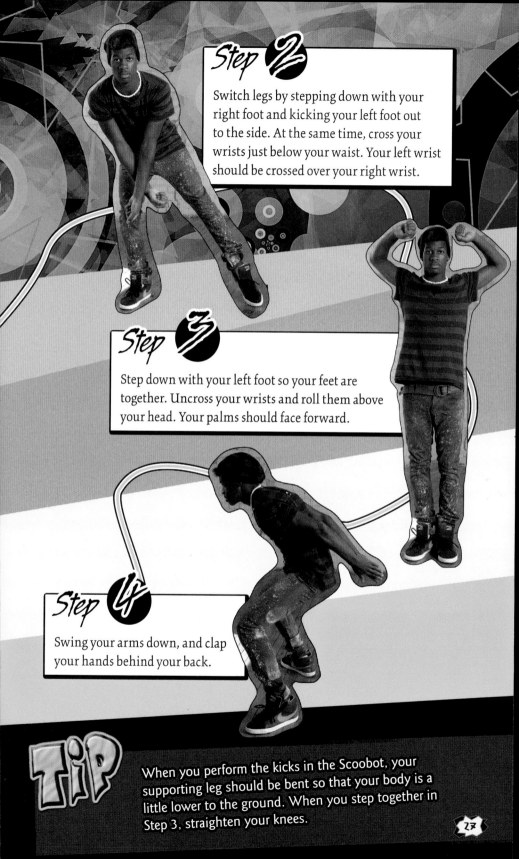

Step 2

Switch legs by stepping down with your right foot and kicking your left foot out to the side. At the same time, cross your wrists just below your waist. Your left wrist should be crossed over your right wrist.

Step 3

Step down with your left foot so your feet are together. Uncross your wrists and roll them above your head. Your palms should face forward.

Step 4

Swing your arms down, and clap your hands behind your back.

Tip

When you perform the kicks in the Scoobot, your supporting leg should be bent so that your body is a little lower to the ground. When you step together in Step 3, straighten your knees.

Scoobot To The Floor

DIFFICULTY: ★★★

Have you mastered the Scoobot? Then it's time to try the Scoobot to the Floor! This **variation** of the Scoobot brings you down to the ground and back up. You'll perform this move in almost the same time it takes you to do the original Scoobot!

Step 1

Repeat Step 1 of the Scoobot. Stand with your feet together. Your arms are by your sides with hands in fists. Kick your right leg to the side. Keep your leg angled toward the ground. At the same time, roll your left wrist up above your head, and extend your right arm out to the right.

variation—*something that is slightly different from another thing of the same type*

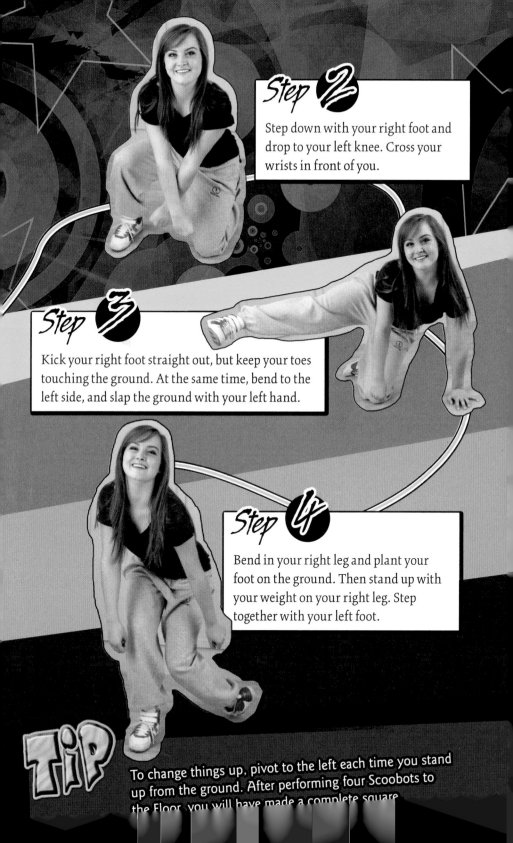

Step ②

Step down with your right foot and drop to your left knee. Cross your wrists in front of you.

Step ③

Kick your right foot straight out, but keep your toes touching the ground. At the same time, bend to the left side, and slap the ground with your left hand.

Step ④

Bend in your right leg and plant your foot on the ground. Then stand up with your weight on your right leg. Step together with your left foot.

Tip

To change things up, pivot to the left each time you stand up from the ground. After performing four Scoobots to the Floor, you will have made a complete square.

Skeeter Rabbit

DIFFICULTY: ★★★

The Skeeter Rabbit is a famous locking move that combines hops and shuffles. James "Skeeter Rabbit" Higgins invented the move in the early 1970s. This step can be performed both to the front and to the side. In this step-by-step instruction, you'll learn how to perform the Skeeter Rabbit to the front.

Step 1

Stand in a relaxed position with your feet close together. Lift your right knee, and then kick forward with your right foot. At the same time, lift your left hand to about waist height.

Step 2

Place your right foot on the floor next to your left one. Drop your left arm. Don't put any weight on the right foot because you'll be picking it back up again.

Step 3

Hop forward onto your right foot and slide your left foot back. Land with your knees bent and feet apart. Most of your weight should be on your right foot. As you do this, lift your right arm to waist height.

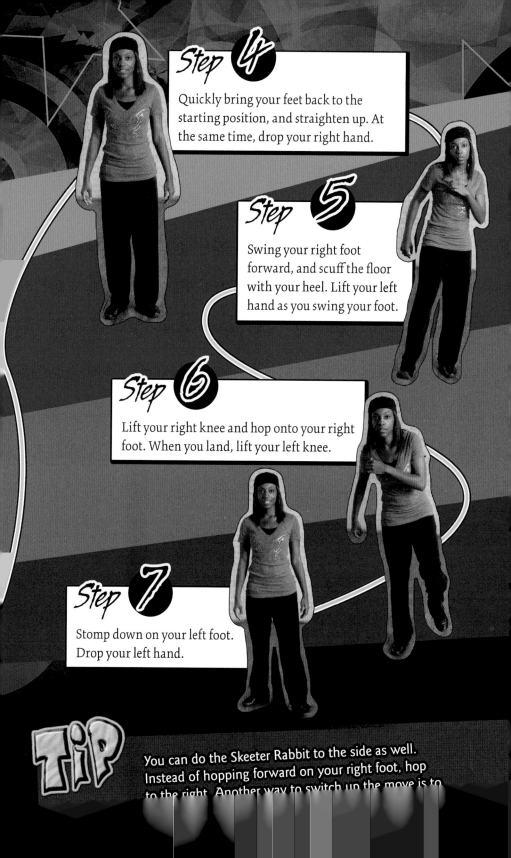

Step 4

Quickly bring your feet back to the starting position, and straighten up. At the same time, drop your right hand.

Step 5

Swing your right foot forward, and scuff the floor with your heel. Lift your left hand as you swing your foot.

Step 6

Lift your right knee and hop onto your right foot. When you land, lift your left knee.

Step 7

Stomp down on your left foot. Drop your left hand.

TiP

You can do the Skeeter Rabbit to the side as well. Instead of hopping forward on your right foot, hop to the right. Another way to switch up the move is to

THE ROBOT

The robot is a funky dance style that developed around the same time as popping and locking. When roboting, dancers copy the stiff movements of robots.

Dime Stop

DIFFICULTY: ★★

The Dime Stop is one of the most important moves you can learn in order to master the robot technique. You can apply the Dime Stop to arm, forearm, or even hip movements. The key is to appear as though you are stopping on a dime with each move of your body.

Arms

Step 1

Stand with your feet shoulder-width apart. Bend your elbows and tuck them into your hips. Your arms are bent at 90-degree angles. Your palms face each other.

Step 2

Keeping your arms bent, raise your left arm up so that your hand is about level with your face. Make sure your palm stays facing to the right. When you end the movement, stop for a beat before continuing. Then raise your right arm. Think of this as your "robot stance."

Forearms

Step 1

Stand with your feet shoulder-width apart and your arms straight out to the sides. Your palms should face forward.

Step 2

Keeping your arms in place, bend your elbows and raise your forearms about 45 degrees. When you end the movement, do not budge from your spot. Tighten your arm muscles and stop for a moment before continuing to Step 3.

Step 3

Raise your forearms a bit more so that your arms are at 90-degree angles. Apply the Dime Stop to the end of your movement by tightening the muscles and staying still.

To look truly robotic, keep your arms and your body completely stiff between your Dime Stops. Don't let your arms, back, hands, or even your neck relax at any point.

Chapter 4

WAVING AND TUTTING

Finger Wave

DIFFICULTY: ⭐⭐

Are you ready to make waves? The Finger Wave makes it look as though a small wave is moving through your hands. You'll be raising and lowering each finger, one after the other.

Step 1

Start with your hands side by side in fists. Tuck your thumbs into your fists. Press together the pointer finger sides of your hands.

Step 2

To start the wave on your left side, lift your left pinky finger.

Step 3

Move the wave through your ring finger and middle finger. As you lower each finger, raise the next one up.

Step 4

Move the wave through your pointer fingers. When you lower your left pointer finger, lift the pointer finger of your right hand.

Step 5

Move the wave all the way to the end by finally lowering the right pinky finger. Repeat the wave coming from the right side by lifting the right pinky finger first.

 **Tip**

The Finger Wave should move quickly through your hands. Don't raise and lower each finger one at a time. Instead, as you raise your pinky finger, your ring finger should already be rising up. The same goes for all of your fingers.

Tutting Combination

DIFFICULTY: ★☆

Tutting is a dance that looks like the poses found on ancient Egyptian art. The style is all about arm movements performed at 90-degree angles. Below is a sample of an eight-count combination using a variety of different positions. Each step is one count.

Step 1

Raise your arms out to the sides. Bend your elbows to create two box shapes. Your hands should be up by your head and flexed at 90-degree angles to your arms. Your palms face down, and your fingers point away from your body.

Step 2

Rotate your hands around so that your palms face the ceiling. Your fingers are still pointing away from you. Maintain the 90-degree angle with your arms.

Step 3

Turn your left hand so the fingers point toward your body. At the same time, turn your head to the right.

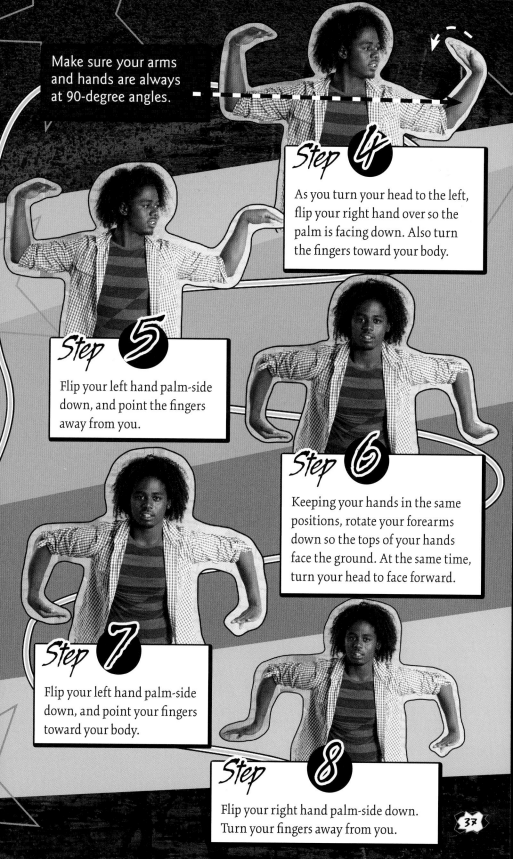

Make sure your arms and hands are always at 90-degree angles.

Step 4

As you turn your head to the left, flip your right hand over so the palm is facing down. Also turn the fingers toward your body.

Step 5

Flip your left hand palm-side down, and point the fingers away from you.

Step 6

Keeping your hands in the same positions, rotate your forearms down so the tops of your hands face the ground. At the same time, turn your head to face forward.

Step 7

Flip your left hand palm-side down, and point your fingers toward your body.

Step 8

Flip your right hand palm-side down. Turn your fingers away from you.

GLIDING, FLOATING, AND SLIDING

BackSlide

DIFFICULTY: ⭐⭐

Also known as the Moonwalk, this famous move features an illusion of the feet. When performed correctly, it looks as though you are walking forward but the ground is pulling you backward. Get ready to amaze your friends!

Step 1

Stand with feet together and your right heel raised.

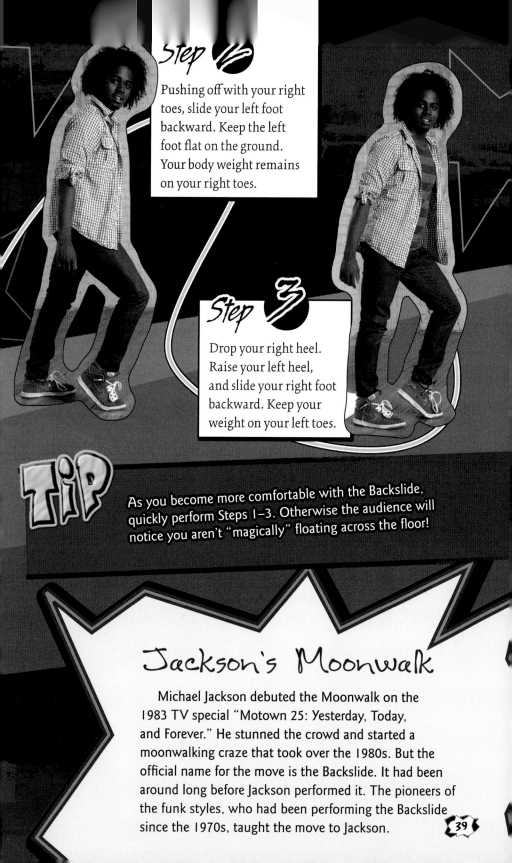

Step 2

Pushing off with your right toes, slide your left foot backward. Keep the left foot flat on the ground. Your body weight remains on your right toes.

Step 3

Drop your right heel. Raise your left heel, and slide your right foot backward. Keep your weight on your left toes.

Tip

As you become more comfortable with the Backslide, quickly perform Steps 1–3. Otherwise the audience will notice you aren't "magically" floating across the floor!

Jackson's Moonwalk

Michael Jackson debuted the Moonwalk on the 1983 TV special "Motown 25: Yesterday, Today, and Forever." He stunned the crowd and started a moonwalking craze that took over the 1980s. But the official name for the move is the Backslide. It had been around long before Jackson performed it. The pioneers of the funk styles, who had been performing the Backslide since the 1970s, taught the move to Jackson.

Side Glide

DIFFICULTY: ★★☆

The Side Glide is a move that sounds harder than it actually is. Once you get the hang of it, you'll be bopping from heel to toe in no time.

Step 1

Stand with toes facing each other.

Step 2

Lift your right heel and your left toes. Turn your toes out. Your weight should be on your right toes and your left heel.

Step 3

Turn both feet in again and drop your heel and toes. Your feet should be flat on the ground.

Step 4

Lift your left heel and your right toes. Turn your toes out. Your weight should be on your left toes and your right heel.

Step 5

Repeat Step 3.

Tip

Try not to overthink this move. Once you get the hang of it, it will feel natural to switch back and forth between heels and toes on both feet.

Chest Float

DIFFICULTY: ★★★

The Chest Float is another type of illusion move. When performed correctly, it looks like your chest drives the movement of your feet. Leave audience members scratching their heads as you float across the dance floor.

Step 1

Stand with your toes facing each other. Put your left hand on the left side of your chest. Push your chest as far to the right as possible. At the same time, put your right hand on your right hip. Push your hips to the left.

Step 2

Switch your arms. Your right hand is now on your chest, and your left hand is on your hip.

Step 3

Push your chest to the left and your hips to the right. As you push your hips, Side Glide to the right.

Check out pages 40–41 for the Side Glide steps.

Tip

You should feel a little strain in your stomach as your chest and hips pull in opposite directions.

The Glide is a footwork illusion similar to the Backslide. It looks like a smooth slide from side to side. But in reality it's all about transferring weight from foot to foot.

GLide

DIFFICULTY:

Step 1

Stand with feet together and toes turned out. Lift your right heel, and put your weight on your right toes. Slide your left foot out to the left. You should end up in a lunge position.

Step 2

In the lunge position, drop your right heel. Lift your left heel. At the same time, turn in your toes.

Turn your toes in so your feet look pigeon-toed.

Step 3

Slide the right foot next to your left foot, and drop the left heel.

Step 4 *not shown*

Repeat Steps 1–3. To reverse the Glide, lift your left heel and slide out with the right foot.

TIP

To make the Glide look continuous, switch positions quickly. As soon as your right foot is next to your left in Step 3, push your weight back onto your right toe, and turn your knee out. Now you can slide out your left foot and begin again.

PRACTICE, PRACTICE, PRACTICE

Now you've learned moves from six different funk styles! If you have trouble remembering them at first, don't give up. With a lot of practice, you can become a master of funk.

agility (uh-GI-luh-tee)—the ability to move fast and easily

battle (BAT-uhl)—a competition between individual dancers or groups; the dancers who receive the loudest crowd applause win

funk styles (FUNK STILEZ)—an umbrella term for many different types of West Coast hip-hop dances, including popping and locking

hamstring (HAM-string)—a muscle in the back of the thigh that helps to flex and extend the leg

illusion (i-LOO-zhuhn)—something that appears to be real but isn't

isolate (EYE-suh-late)—to highlight a particular muscle or area of the body separate from the others

limber (LIM-bur)—bending or moving easily

pendulum (PEN-juh-luhm)—a weight in a clock that moves from side to side and helps keep the clock ticking regularly

pivot (PIV-uht)—to turn suddenly as if on a central point

quadriceps (KWAH-druh-seps)—a muscle in the front part of the thigh

transition (tran-ZISH-uhn)—a step performed in order to move from one dance step to another

variation (vair-ee-AY-shuhn)—something that is slightly different from another thing of the same type

Cornish, Melanie J. *The History of Hip Hop.* Crabtree Contact. New York: Crabtree Pub., 2009.

Fitzgerald, Tamsin. *Hip-Hop and Urban Dance.* Dance. Chicago: Heinemann Library, 2009.

Freese, Joan. *Hip-Hop Dancing.* Dance. Mankato, Minn.: Capstone Press, 2008.

Garofoli, Wendy. *Hip-Hop Dancing Volume 2: Breaking.* Hip-Hop Dancing. Mankato, Minn.: Capstone Press, 2011.

INTERNET SITES

FactHound offers a safe, fun way to find Internet sites related to this book. All of the sites on FactHound have been researched by our staff.

Here's all you do:

Visit *www.facthound.com*

Type in this code: 9781429654869

Backslide, 38–39
boogaloo (dance style), 11

Campbell, Don, 4, 21
Chest Float, 42–43
clothing, 6, 7

Dime Stops, 32–33

Electric Boogaloos, 11

Finger Wave, 34–35
funk dance styles, 5, 6, 7, 8, 39, 45
funk music, 6

gear, 6
Glide, 44–45

Higgins, James "Skeeter Rabbit," 30

Jackson, Michael, 39

locking
     history of, 4, 6, 7, 21, 30

Moonwalk. *See* Backslide
muscle isolations, 8, 15, 17

Neck-o-Flex, 10–11, 16

Old Man, 11, 18–19

popping
     history of, 4, 6, 7, 11

roboting (dance style), 5, 32

Scoobot, 26–27, 28
Scoobot to the Floor, 28–29
Scooby Doo, 22–23
Side Glide, 40–41
Skeeter Rabbit, 30–31
Solomon, Sam "Boogaloo Sam," 4, 11
strengthening, 9
stretching, 8
strobing, 14–15

tutting, 5, 36–37
Twist-o-Flex, 16–17

Walkout, 12–13
Whichaway, 24–25
Wrist Twirls, 20–21